Just Love Me

B.A. Crews

PublishAmerica
Baltimore

First printing

To Tim

Enjoy the Journey!

You are such a Cutie (Cutie)

B Crews

ISBN: 1-4137-2509-0
PUBLISHED BY PUBLISHAMERICA, LLLP
www.publishamerica.com
Baltimore

Printed in the United States of America

This book is dedicated to Cheryl.

Acknowledgments

How do you thank all of the people that are and have been in your life? Hopefully, the presence of these pages will touch on it. The lessons learned the hard way and easy way from days of extreme loneliness to a voice from God saying your life will soon be free. To days of thinking I should save the world only to be given a prayer placed in the palm of my hand by this wonderful woman. A newspaper clipping beginning with "Slow me down Lord; ease the pounding of my heart by the quieting of my mind. Teach me the art of taking minute vacations."

I thank my friends and family who are and have been such an important part of my life. Accepting three a.m. phone calls without complaint to celebrating victories in my life to taking on the defeated moments and making them easier to bear; I have been blessed beyond measure. The magic of my life has taught me to be able to feel more, see more, do more, and take risks.

Special attention to Ginger Johnson for her designs and creativity in formatting *Just Love Me*.

Sheri Paulk and Dean Smith for illustrations

Caryn, Chris, Kay, Ruth, D.H., Sandy, Sandra Gail, Sue, Patty, and everyone who was instrumental in helping me to live the dream.

Thanks for believing in the magic.

Foreword

How do you sum up a life in so many pieces of scrap paper?

A life born out of pain, joy, and the never ending search for a quiet place to lay your head and rest your heart.

I have no regrets—only experiences that have left me still full of wonder and an incredible capacity to love over and over again.

I have found that life is made up of moments well lived or unnoticed. I have found that we do not try hard enough to keep the love that we have. We are restless and we are always trying to find ourselves. Go look in the mirror and save yourself and someone else the pain of the realization that what you left behind may be the very thing you need. Take time to unclutter your mind from the day's events, whether they may be trials or tribulations or joys and exhilaration.

Be glad for the day and celebrate it—it may be your last.

Take the time to tell the people you love that you love them over and over again. Never grow weary of reaching out to others, because in reaching out your arms you will shut out the wolves that come at us to take away the goodness. Make a circle with your family and friends and drive the wolves away with your smiles.

Be glad for the day and celebrate it—it may be your last.

I can only hope that the loves of my life, my friends and family will remember me on a warm sunny day in spring when everything becomes new, as I will remember them. I salute the ones who have broken my heart, the ones who tried to mend it, and the one who arrived to fill it. Wishing all of you all the beautiful things you are and have been to me.

The Jesus Chair

Hey! Before you go running off thinking
this is about religion just come and sit for a minute
in the Jesus chair.

Imagine sitting in the lap of God.
Imagine that you have been given
the power to help change the world and
then DO IT.

Arm yourself with smiles and kind words
Pass them on, give them away
They will come back to you.
Then when you have been rejected
Time after time
You keep going back
until someone smiles just to get rid of you.

Pay attention to the people around you
The ones in your lives almost daily.
Praise the ones that smile
Pray for the ones that don't.

Find renewal and comfort in
your own chair because
God is everywhere we want him to be.
Imagine your chair is the Jesus chair
Feel the hand of God leading you
out as His messenger.

Imagine how important
You are!

I Remember

I remember cardboard houses
Eating mud pies
out behind the old oak tree
Tomato fights
Chocolate bars
Hide and go seek
The mystery of stealing kumquats
from behind the funeral home
with a boy named Buddy Taylor.

The let down when I got
a Cinderella watch
instead of a Mickey Mouse.

I was the best marble shooter
on the block
and all of the boys disliked me because I beat them.

How tough I thought I was
with my Hop-A-Long Cassidy jacket
and six gun shooter
while all my girlfriends were off
playing with
their "squeeze me and I cry" dolls.

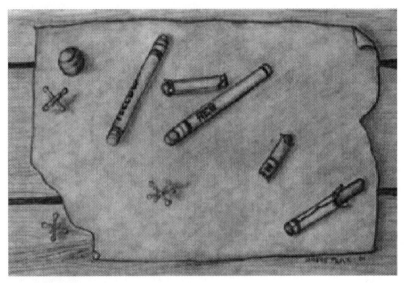

My first kiss
was from underneath the bed
as my friend and I were searching
for the ball that went with my jacks.

How funny it felt
but how excited I was
about getting away with something or
someone.

There was high school
and all the girls in their new clothes
and me in my hand-me-downs.
I was never included in anything.
I was chosen the one
with the best sense of humor.

I never knew if I was being laughed at
Or with, but always remained funny.
In basketball practice
they all snickered
when my made-up bra
which was nothing more
than an old strapless bathing suit top
fell down
how embarrassed I was.
I wanted to run and hide
and how much I disliked my grandmother
for making me wear it.
She never knew.

I remember my first love
the funny feeling
in the pit of my stomach.
How soft and warm I felt
and how lucky I was to be so important
to someone.

I remember kick-the-can, hopscotch,
hide and go seek, and 25-cent movies.
There was the imaginary taxicab
I made out of three chairs
that took my friends and me
to far away places,
like Florida…and still do.

My plastic magic wand
and all the power I had to banish
all the things that
made me sad and cried…and still try.

I remember the first note
passed to me and hoped it was
someone saying, "I love you."
I remember the reaction
on my grandmother's face
and realized it meant nothing.

The pigtails
Being chosen to be the Indian maiden
in the school play.
How the Croker sack costume
made me itch but how proud I was to be
singled out from everyone else.

I remember the Indian lullaby I sang
and how quiet everything was.
How nervous I felt
as I picked out a hole in the ceiling
because all my friends were there to
make me laugh and spoil
my big moment if I looked at them.
I thought my voice crackled
and I had ruined it all.
Then it was over and I heard
the applause
and knew I had made it.
How I cried because the people
I loved most stayed at home.
They never knew.

I remember fighting with a boy
because he picked on
the loneliest girl in class.
His mom called my mom and said
I broke two ribs.
How was I to know he had chalk bones?
Always the protector.

In the sixth grade I was chosen to sing
 "Sixteen Tons" when the class
became unruly.
After all of these years, I'm still another
day older and deeper in debt.

I remember my first shots for school.
How my grandmother made a sling for
my wounded arm and placed me on
a pallet so I could be near her
in the kitchen.
I remember the kitchen sounds,
how safe and secure I felt.
I remember Kool-Aid and lemonade.

I remember swapping comic books
The excitement when someone
on the block got a TV
and we all crowded around and watched
Ed Sullivan.

Ponytails and how I hated crinoline slips
and the boys always pulling them down.

I remember feather beds
and hot water bottles,
and wood burning stoves.
Snuggling from the cold and listening
to the rain on the tin roof
that serenaded me into sleep.

I have loved and lost so many times that
I seem to have spent most of
my life in the middle
never knowing if I was lost or found.

Rain

The rain flows down
the windowpane
in uneven patterns,
so like the life we have come
to know
 as our own.
Dramatic, like a play
where you anticipate
the curtain going up
and with it the masks
 we wear throughout the day.
Some, all our lives and
with it the hope that when
the masks are removed
someone will take us as we
really are
and not
for who
we appear
to be.

We Are

We are the Writers, Artists, Musicians, and Dancers.
We are, I believe, a lonely happy bunch
our talent seemingly our best that we offer.
Everyone amazed at our ability to expose ourselves
as we dance across the stage of our life.
We are envious that we are not
content to be satisfied with a beer and a ballgame
Constantly we try to seek out beauty and truth
and give it away
We fear rejection
We become even better at our trade
We are intense yet we seek simplicity
We are travelers waiting and seeking
to end the journey
or are we content with our lives as they are?
With our gathered up talked about moments
perhaps spent trying to show others
that the moment is all we have.

Fantasies & Dreams

I'm not sure when I went into my imaginary world.
I only know I never came out, nor do I wish to.
I have found relief in the humor of our lives.
The choices that we could make but rarely do
My least favorite word is reality—
Fantasies and dreams are my companions
Fighting to survive in a world
That stopped believing in Santa Claus.
Shame on you, for being so grown up!
How could we ever survive without once listening to
"Twas The Night Before Christmas?"

You and I Were Searching

You and I were searching
when we stumbled across each other.

My journey ended with you
Yours began with me.

Leave it to me to be on the right bus
at the wrong time.

Picket Fence

I'm ready for the picket fence
and rosebushes,
bowling on Thursday nights,
washday on Wednesday,
trips to the supermarket
and forty-hour work-weeks.
If you can remember
the candlelight and the roses,
laugh with me,
help me through the bad times
and help me
to make the good times last.

Technicolor Dreams

I watch you sleeping and wonder if you have
Technicolor dreams
of midnight walks in the snow on ice colored nights.

As you stir I wonder if in your dreams
you are reaching out for me on some moonlit night
In some faraway place
like your backyard...

I wonder if you dream
of the white horse that whisks us away
on some magical journey.
I look at you and smile
and know that, if need be,
you'll come up with it.

Basketball

The desire to play basketball
Was there but no money for the shoes.
So I borrowed someone's from the locker room—
Always carefully placing them back
I thank whoever you are
you were my friend

My Life

I ask no one's permission for living my life
Unless they are willing to take the mistakes
that go with it…

I Remember Roller Skates

I remember roller skates
And mistakes
Monopoly and Parcheesi
And pick-up sticks
And
1 potato 2 potato 3 potato 4

I remember paper dolls
Crayons and coloring books

You could use whatever color you wanted

There were so many choices—
Unlike the black and white world I grew up in—
Me loving everybody
And being told who to love
And who not to—
I suppose I was a rebel in those days.
Sometimes I think I still am—
Still fighting for the right to love who you choose.

I am sometimes a weary traveler.
I remember roller skates

Dream Big

First comes the dream and
Then the reality of what you
Did with that dream—so
Dream Big

Where Are They Now?

Hula Hoops and Betty Boops
Cookies as big as your face.
Words like Kemosabe and
songs of depth like Sha-La-La-La,
Shoo-Be-Do-Be-Do, Shing-A-Ling-A-Ling.
Questions like who put the Bomp in the Bomp De Bomp
De Bomp?
Who put the ram in the Rama Lama Ding Dong?

I remember slow dancing to "In The Still Of The Night."
Never wanting to stop until my partner asked if
he could lead the next one
The answer was no.

I remember the ice-cream truck and the
screams of joy and excitement
Ice cream! Ice cream!
You could hear the chants two blocks away,
so afraid it would leave. I don't know what
horrible trauma it may have caused if we missed it.
Ring on!

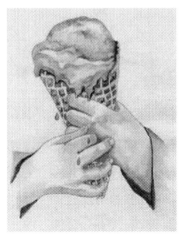

YOUR SMILE

Your
smile
is going
to get
you
arrested!

You Take Hold of Me

You take hold of me as if I were a fine instrument
in need of being tuned.

You stroke and play me well.

I think you need to get your hands insured.

Butterfly

I saw you today in what seemed like a brief encounter
But then all encounters seem brief with butterflies.
You being elusive
My feeling intrusive
But yet in a short amount of time
I think we both came away being the student more so than the teacher
Two old souls
Brought together to share journeys
Me perhaps looking for a place to lay my head
and rest my heart.
I think somehow I knew you had landed somewhere
I am glad that it was a safe landing.
As for me
the journey continues.

The Phone Call

If you're calling me up to make up,
well you can just hang up…

In a few minutes.

Let Go

I let you go today
Not because there was another person
but because we live in different worlds.

You must go to a safe place
There you will find the love of your life—Yourself.

I cannot escape the world I live in.
I live around wolves not of my choosing.

I am a weary traveler searching always to find
someone
who has let go of
the past that clutters your mind and is passed on
to another person

We all have something in our past that we try and
 hang on to
Let go and embrace the day
It is the only one you have
So live the moment without guarantee there will be
 another
It is not to be wasted
and no one needs to be punished for your mistakes
and past.

We all have our own.

Your Forecast

You are windy

Slightly cool

Warm

Never cold

You must have known I hated
Winter alone

The Wolves

The wolves are coming—
disguised as jealousy,
doubt,
loneliness
and fear.
They are barking at the moon
that lights up the night.
Here for no good
Just to give you a fright
But I am the Master
and I've got a plan
We'll run them out of town
'cause I know
we can.

The Storm

How can you
ever be the CALM
in the midst of the
STORM,

Until you have entered
THE STORM?

Hanging In

We spend so much time getting in and over
things;
Whatever Happened to

HANGING IN and HANGING ON?

Found

I looked for you
Until you found

Me

Meditation

The sun dances across the river like diamonds
As your eyes glance my way and dance across my heart.
You pause as if in need of meditation
And I wander away to let you wonder…

Thoughts

Peace is not something we look for...

but something we take with us...

Think about where you are going
Instead of where you've been

Under Suspicion

Anyone with a SMILE on their face
is under suspicion

Masterpiece

I could sculpt you with
my eyes closed.
I have traced your body
and perhaps your mind
so many times with
just my fingertips that
when the masterpiece that is you
is undraped, it will have been
created from this feeling called Love.

My Lover

There are six words to describe
my lover

Uh uh uh uh uh—uhmmm

Amazing

The first time I saw you I thought your eyes were
amazing
They still are only now you know.

I found your innocence of life refreshing
Your sense of love, responsibility and obligation
to family respectful and amazing

I found your tired but beautiful smile amazing.

I found your love and tenderness, touching,
healing, and amazing.

I found your ventures into uncharted territories
which is Life about to be amazing

I found your quietness mysterious and amazing

I found your recognition of making
Time for yourself, new and amazing

I find you growing and changing willing
to run with the tide wherever it
may take you—That is amazing

I see you for all of the beautiful things
that you are about to become
Amazing

I hope that you will learn to open
up and find yourself as amazing
as I do…

The Fixer

Well, here you go again.

The Fixer

Ready to seek out
To solve and make better
the hurts
of any and all victims
who have been wounded by this thing called
Love & Life.

Here you go

The Magician

Pulling out tricks and fantasies
to sell to anyone
who has a need to believe in the possibilities
that the world may be a fun place after all.

And here I am
waiting again for someone who doesn't need fixing,
for someone who has their own magic
And someone to love me easy…

Free

I'm beginning to think we should love
for the moment, because once
we start asking for more—
we get less.

At the beginning we give so freely
and then we began to demand
what is already there.
We have to be free to love.

First you must enter my mind
Before you touch my heart
And remember
My body is extra

Your touch is a language
Without words

You are the dream
that stepped
out of my head
and entered my heart

Conversations without Words

I remember feeling uncomfortable
and when you looked away
I knew we were losing each other.

Third Degree Burns

If hurt could be measured in degrees
This would have been
a third degree burn.

Thought

My therapist at Christmas
treating me for a broken heart
asked me if I was suicidal.
I said I didn't know it was an option.

Lost and Found

Don't lose yourself
while trying to find yourself.

In My Mind

If you were only in my mind,
I could think you away;
but you're in my heart,
so it will take longer.

Today

Today is the only day we have.
We can live it or
we can waste it.

Nite-Lite

Now that you're here
I don't think I will be needing
my nite-lite.

Give Yourself a Kiss

Give yourself a kiss today
Just turn your lips inside out
and really give yourself a **SMACK**
No, no, no, silly...
not **THAT** way.
Oh, never mind...

*Kiss **ME** instead*

Negative or Positive

You say you're NEGATIVE
And I say I'm POSITIVE
Just want you to know
That you can't start without
me.

Never Let You Go

I could never let you go as sure
as I could ignore the sun
or the moon
or the stars
that I have seen in your eyes

I could never let you go as sure
as I could hold a deaf ear to the music
in my life like the sound of your voice.

I could never let you go as sure
as the warmth in your smile
or the look on your face
when we are alone—

I could never let you go
even if the wolves
came I would fight to
the death and breath for
the love of you
for another day…

Drowning

I look your way and you look away.
This time it's really going to hurt.
The tears are going to come.
I can swallow them and drown
or let them flow and stand naked before
you.

I

t
h
i
n
k

I'll
drown.

Waiting

I unlocked the door and gave you the key;
I tore down the wall and built you a bridge;
But, you never came.
Maybe tomorrow…

Taking Time

If you would take the time to take care of
your needs,
you will probably be
taking care
of
mine...

Which Is Worse?

I can't tell which is worse:
The pain of losing you,
or the pain of being in love

all by myself...

Your Hands

When I think of you
I think of your hands
and how gently
they glide over me
as if I were a fine painting
being drawn from memory…

I Remember Bar Harbor

I remember Bar Harbor, Maine
A dream come true
More beautiful than I imagined.
I remember the cottage where we stayed
Lace curtains,
Neatly stacked wood for the fire place
Tomato soup
Lobster

The whaleboat
and how I had a nausea coma
the whole trip but I did catch
the tail of a whale at 09:00.

I remember being so happy
sharing all this splendor
with wonderful friends

22 hours on a train
loving every minute
loving you
every second…

Flight to Freedom

I hope one day, my love,
in your flight for freedom
you will circle over me
and if you find me to your liking,
ask me to join you
and end the search.
If not, I wish for you a safe landing
somewhere…

Why?

I don't need this aggravation.
"You deserve so much better than me."
"You are so wonderful, talented, and beautiful,
and let's not forget—
kind."
So I want to ask you,
If I am all of these things,
Why are you leaving?

Convertible Hair

You've got legs into infinity
and convertible hair
A smile you can't just get anywhere
Your voice is soft.
Your word is true.
Everyone you meet gets a crush on you.
I always have to worry when they will drop the bomb
asking me if I'm your Mom.
Actually I don't think you're all
that cute all dressed up in
your designer suit
You go in the Minute Markets
or anywhere suddenly the
Universe is totally aware
that it's Peggy Sue
with the convertible hair.

Let Your Eyes Speak

Sometimes I think your eyes
must be connected to your heart
and your mouth
to your mind.

Sometimes I wish you would close your mouth
and let your eyes speak.

I Wonder

I wonder if anyone ever waited on phone calls

I never made

or visits

that never came

I wonder if you have such a need for me...

A love so right
even a flaw can be a renewal.

Ghosts

Ghosts from the past
Ghosts from the present
All in your mind—you live in a beautiful haunted house.
You are restless;
The search is there to find out what is real or unreal.
Your world is unfinished business
Would you be satisfied to answer the questions in your heart?

If

If you are going to be distracted let it be me
If I've ever done anything right in my life
let it be you...

If I Changed

Would you like me better if I changed the color of my eyes?
If I didn't squeeze the toothpaste in the middle?
Or turn the stereo up too loud?
Maybe if I had curls?
Or laughed less?
Was more serious?
Or gave up softball and took a class on how to be proper?
Maybe you would like me better if I was someone else.

Maybe you should find someone else
because
softball is too big a sacrifice...

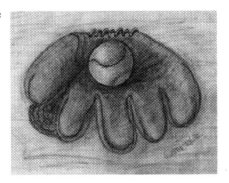

Color Blind

I thought you gave me a green light.

You said it was red.

Can I help it if I'm color blind?

Can You Speak to Me?

In later years, I would know and understand
how much my mother loved me...To have taken me to safety,
and to run for her life from someone
I never knew (my father)...this is for all of us.

Can you speak to me?

Can you speak to me softly, but strongly?

Can you touch me without bruising?

Can you recognize the need in my eyes?

When the words don't come

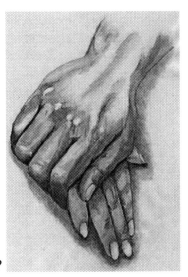

Can you know when I am growing?

Allowing enough room.

Can you move with me and not against me?

Can you want me standing up, as much as
lying down?

Can you, in all of this,
love me in the fashion of which I am not
accustomed to?

ALIVE!

I have held the sun in my fingertips
sent my dreams out
on the wings of birds
I have created smiles
by just giving one
I have played in the autumn leaves
Touched the stars simply by reaching out
and knowing that they are reachable
My hands caress the day
knowing this
by letting go of the things that bind me.

I AM
ALIVE!

If for Some Reason
When the Lights Go Out

If for some reason the lights go out of the sun,
God can always use the fire in your eyes
and the warmth in your smile
to serve the purpose.

Not by Chance

We met not by chance not to
be put off until all is right
with the rest of the world.

We say we know each other but
yet we are apart, separated,
awaiting some false approval.

We came together in a world of two
I have stood naked before you
in thoughts and dreams.

We must come together soon
and apologize for wandering away
You must come to me now.

The hands of time will attempt
to blow away the delicate petals of our lives
I can no longer fantasize you when I know
you are real.

Growing Up

So what are the perks for
Growing up?

Please note this page is blank.

If I Were Cleopatra

I remember once with a group of people
You were talking of pyramids
And I was sitting there wishing I were Cleopatra

You talked of friends who traveled
And how brave they were

You talked of music and meditation,
Of once wanting to be a hippie
And I realized that you had yet to experience
Your own fantasy, so I asked that you and I go away
In search of our own
And you ran and I went away in hopes you would
Follow
And bought a place that gave you a piece of the ocean
So sure you would come.

Then you called and we talked and you asked the
Ouija board
If we would ever be together again
And of course it answered "no."

God, I give up.
How can you fight that?

Working Christmas

Why is it we only remember holidays
When some middle-of-the-week day would
Do?
Besides, I have to work Christmas!

Risks

You have been conditioning
Yourself to doing without
This thing called love.
And I have been preparing myself
For the time when I would
Find it.
Even though there is a
Risk involved maybe we will
Have learned something new
From each other.

Caress the Day

Run your fingertips across
The sun and feel the warmth
Reach way up high and touch

The stars

Go ahead and look for the
Light of day and keep pushing the

Dark clouds away

The day is filled with endless possibilities.

Ode to John Wayne / Sissy Girl

Blue jean skirt, flashing eyes
Either way she can tantalize
A smile that out warms the sun

Riding her horse packing a gun
She can be tough as nails
or tender as night

She's John Wayne / Sissy Girl
and she's doing awright

John Wayne / Sissy Girl
Once tried to eat a cactus because
she thought that would be something
John would do
and it hurt and then she cried.

She is still my hero.

*You can be erased and
Replaced with 12 ice cream
Sandwiches and Neopolitan*

It's Raining

It's raining want to meet me on the sidewalk?
We can meet under an umbrella
Or get reckless. Abandon good sense
And skip in the puddles.
Laugh out loud as lovers do.

Anything but this LOUD silence.
Anything except the sadness I hear in you voice.
Try and remember what we were and what we are
And what we will be.

It's raining will you meet me on the sidewalk?
Will you meet me halfway? Please.
The weather forecast depends
On your smile

Forgive Me

While I was off preaching peace and harmony

You were tapping me on the shoulder
Trying to alert me of your feelings
I thinking surely you have everything you need; failed to hear and feel
The importance it deserved when the
Tapping took place and more than once
In my arrogance at thinking I could
"Fix It" made it worse by denying
The existence of any problem. My thinking
It would go away—I failed you and pray that You will Forgive me and
Remember who I am before you
Are afraid to tap on my shoulder again
I will be paying attention...

One on One

It is my birthday and I am alone
Starting to believe that's how it's going
To be
Great at loving the world no good
At one on one
I have been busy all my life reaching out
To other people and when you
Reached out for me you thought
I wasn't there by the sound of your voice
You aren't there. You were my Dream
That I held in my hands that slipped away
from me that has to come back willingly
Too Beautiful to demand
Please love me unafraid
So I can know what it is to love
One on one...I need the experience

Come Let's Dance!

I'm the one with the white fringe
Turn down the lights and turn up the music
My theme song "What Becomes of the Brokenhearted" driving me on.
For a few hours I will dance for you and make you feel special.
Bring your change, fill the jukebox with
quarters, punch those numbers and
watch me go.
Just give me an audience and I'll take you
for a ride.
Come one come all whoever wants to hide.
In the background playing is "I'll Be There" and
if you are lucky tonight it will be
you that is chosen to speak with me
for awhile.

No touching allowed!

Giving love has always been easy for me.
Giving my heart is another thing.
My whole life has been a stage.
Time to come down and enjoy the dance.

All I ever needed was you.

Come let's dance!

1966

When I Think of You

When I think of you I think how lucky I am
to have you as a friend, always unselfishly
listening to everyone's problems and
concerns and making them more important
than your own

Giving out words of wisdom and hope with
a never-ending supply of comfort.
If I could grant a wish it would be that
everything you give away will come back to
you. After coming to know you I have
realized that you have added to my life as I
hope I have yours. If I could manufacture
your smile the world would cease to have
anything to bitch about.

We would lie in hammocks and dream lofty
dreams, paint our names across the sky in
pastels and pink hues.

I know what it is to be blessed, to call your
name and think of you.

Listen to the Rain

I was sitting by the window listening to
the sounds of rain. I love the rain.

It's as if the heavens open up,
cleansing the earth, running us in doors
I think on purpose to slow us down
to make us melancholy and still.

I can hear the melodic sounds on the
tin roof as it teases me into slumber.

The plants and flowers become alive
perhaps we should do the same.

Listen to the rain.

Stop!

Did you see the sun coming up to beckon
you to a new day?

Even if you can't see the sun, it is always
there, maybe peeping out from the
horizon to spy on us.

Sometimes I think it's God's flashlight
giving us the light of day to prepare for
the night.

One more chance to stop and pay
attention to your life.

Come and Play with Me

Come and play with me
Show me the hummingbirds
the orchids
daisies and lilies.
Let's stand and stare at the clearing
await the deer.
Show me your garden, the sweat of your brow.
Show me the chipmunks.
Show me your smile.
Show me everything I didn't see
with you across the miles.
Show me your hammock where you dream your dreams
I'll show you magic
Music,
Meditation,
Pink roses,
Sandy beaches,
Sandpipers,
Coffee breaks that last until noon.
I'll show you dreams you never thought possible.
I'll take you in my imaginary cab to an address nobody knows
I'll hold you captive with chocolate,
fluffy clouds, kisses,
stars so big they light up the night.
I'll give you fireflies, show you my shiny marbles.
We will share the wonder of it all.
Come and play with me.
Please?

The Dream

As the rain flows down the windowpane
I watch you sleeping by the glow
of a flickering candle nearing its end.

I notice the light as it catches
your hair and you stir
as if a dream has entered your sleep.
A soft murmur escapes your lips
I wonder if you are in a childlike dream of innocence.
The way we felt
when we first met.

I've walked the earth much longer
trying to imagine you as you are in this moment
when the world is forbidden to intrude.
I wrote of you then
as I do now
of teaching you that
love waits for no one once it is here.

I trace your face with my fingertips
moving across and down your body
Hoping to touch your mind
to reassure you
that the dream is real.

Live your life as if it's temporary
Because it is

to be continued...

Printed in the United States
84770LV00004B/445-498/A